Clara
Barton

David R. Collins

Illustrated by
Ken Landgraf

BARBOUR
PUBLISHING, INC.
Uhrichsville, Ohio

© MCMXCIX by Barbour Publishing, Inc.

ISBN 1-57748-601-3

Published by Barbour Publishing, Inc., P.O. Box 719,
Uhrichsville, Ohio 44683 http://www.barbourbooks.com

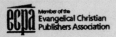
Member of the
Evangelical Christian
Publishers Association

Printed in the United States of America.

Clara
Barton

"DOROTHY, TELL THEM IT'S GOING TO BE A GIRL."

1

Snowflakes danced along the crust of the icy Massachusetts countryside on Christmas Day, 1821. Near the town of Oxford stood a quiet farmhouse. Excitement filled its kitchen.

"I do hope it's a girl!" ten-year-old Sally Barton squealed.

"Well, it's going to be a boy." David Barton winked at his brother Stephen.

"No, it's not," Sally protested. "Dorothy, tell them it's going to be a girl!"

As Dorothy, the oldest of the children, finished washing the last bowl, she handed it to Sally for drying.

"No one should care," Dorothy declared. "It's wonderful enough that it's happening on Christmas."

Wiping her hands, Dorothy sat in front of the fire. Sally, David, and Stephen joined her. Soon all four children were playing games before the crackling logs.

Suddenly the door of the back bedroom opened. A tall, tired man came out and sat in a rocking chair.

"You've got a new sister," he announced.

"A girl–just like I said!" Sally twirled around the room.

Dorothy knelt beside her father. "Have you thought of a name?"

"Your mother and I decided to call her Clarissa Harlowe Barton."

"For Aunt Clarissa?" Stephen asked.

Father nodded.

David shook his head. "It's too long a name for a baby."

"Call her Clara if you like," Father answered.

Clara's early years passed quickly. Though the area had few children her age, she was never alone.

"YOU'VE GOT A NEW SISTER."

While her brothers and sisters were at school, Clara followed her father around their farm.

Clara was her father's pet. Often he would set the dark-haired girl on his lap. Clara loved these times. She knew she would hear the old war stories. As a young man, her father had served his country bravely.

"Tell me again," Clara begged her father often. "Tell me everything you did."

Clara also loved animals. Button, their terrier, was Clara's favorite. They played together by the hour. Mama could never understand how they got so dirty.

Clara was a ball of energy. She begged her brothers and sisters to play with her when they came home from school. But after supper, she became a student.

Dorothy taught Clara to read. Teaching her to write was Sally's job. Math came from Stephen. Mother and Father taught her Bible verses.

Then there was David. "Enough of this book learnin'," he'd say. He showed her how to climb

CLARA PLAYED WITH HER BROTHERS AND SISTERS.

trees, pound nails, and run races. His lessons were always fun.

One day as David and Clara sat on a fence near the meadow, a glistening black colt trotted up to them.

"I think he wants to take someone for a ride," David announced. He hoisted Clara to the colt's back. "Hold on to his mane, little one."

"David, I'm scared. What if I fall?"

"There's only one answer. Don't!" David ran to another colt and jumped on his back. Giving the colt a quick clap on the back, he raced forward, slapping Clara's colt as he passed.

Away they galloped. Clara gripped the mane tightly.

"You're doing fine, Clara!" David cried. He led the way around the meadow several times, then returned to where they had started.

"Whoa!" he bellowed. Both horses jerked to a halt. David sprang down and ran to his sister. "You ride like a champion."

One night after the Bartons finished supper, David

AWAY THEY GALLOPED.

offered to wash dishes.

"Yes, Mama, we can finish these things," said Sally.

Mama shook her head. "There's something strange about all this help."

"Why, Mama," David began, "we just want to–"

"I know," Mama interrupted. "You just *want* something. Sally might volunteer to help, but you, David?"

"But–"

"Oh, let's ask her," Sally said. "Mama, we want to take Clara to school."

"What could a three-year-old girl learn at school?"

"She's almost four!" David exclaimed.

"She's much brighter than most of the children," a proud Sally added.

"Including me!" added David.

"Wait a minute!" Mama exclaimed. "You two are going too fast. A great deal of thought went into this performance."

"Well, we *have* talked about it," replied David.

"MAMA, WE WANT TO TAKE CLARA TO SCHOOL."

"You always say to have reasons for whatever you do."

Mama nodded. "And I also say that whatever you do must make sense. Even if your father and I agree that Clara could go, how would she get there?"

"I could take her!" Stephen sprang up from his place on the hearth.

"Oh, another one is in on this plot. And what about your chores? Your father would never agree if chores were left undone."

"I'd just get up earlier," Stephen said.

Mama could see how badly her children wanted her to say yes.

"If your father agrees, it will be fine with me."

Instantly she was swamped with hugs and kisses. Then the children dashed off to find their father.

"And where are my kitchen helpers now?" Mama asked herself.

The children found Father in the farmyard. He was harder to persuade. Finally he agreed.

On her first day of school, Clara was excited. Off she went, riding high on Stephen's shoulders.

THE CHILDREN FOUND FATHER IN THE FARMYARD.

Sally and David, running ahead, paused now and then to throw snowballs at each other.

Suddenly Clara looked very serious.

"Stephen, I'm frightened. I want to go home."

"Don't you want to learn things?"

"Yes, but I want to do it with you and Sally and everybody at home."

Stephen stopped and let her slip to the ground. He knelt on his knees before her.

"Clara, you learn things fast. You are ready for school. And you'll meet new friends."

"But won't people laugh at me? I want you to be proud of me."

"Clara, we are proud of you. We're glad you're going to school with us." He gave his sister a kiss. "Now let's hurry so we won't be late."

As she entered the schoolhouse, Clara was surprised at how crowded everything was. Seeing a seat in the corner, she ran to it and climbed up. David hurried over to her.

"Clara, you mustn't sit there. That's the dunce's chair."

"STEPHEN, I WANT TO GO HOME."

"What's a dunce?"

"It's a student who doesn't know his lesson. If a student can't answer Colonel Stone's questions, the student must sit on this chair."

Clara jumped down. "I hope I never have to sit there, David. Have you ever had to?"

"Well. . .oh, there's Colonel Stone. You'd better sit up front so he can see you." Clara hurried to one of the front seats. She glanced back to make sure her brothers and sisters were still there. Seeing them gave her courage.

The first day at school slipped by quickly. In spelling, Clara surprised Mr. Stone by knowing third-grade words.

"How did your first day go at school?" Father asked at supper. "Did you have to sit in the dunce chair?"

"She climbed into it the moment she walked into the schoolhouse," David teased.

Clara's face turned red.

"At least she'll never have to sit there because she doesn't know her lesson," Sally replied. "It

"OH, THERE'S COLONEL STONE."

seems to me that you didn't know the third president of the United States, David Barton, and you had to sit—"

"Say, I think I'd better get some more wood for the fire." David grabbed his coat and hurried outside.

As the door slammed, Father roared with laughter. Soon everyone was laughing. And that night every Barton child recited the names of the presidents.

SOON EVERYONE WAS LAUGHING.

"BUT, FATHER, I WOULDN'T BE HAPPY
LIVING ANYWHERE ELSE."

2

One night, Clara was the topic of conversation at supper. Everyone was concerned about her shyness.

"I think it would be best for Clara if she met more people and saw new places," Father said. "Maybe she should go to the Oxford boarding school. She would meet many children her own age."

"But, Father, I wouldn't be happy living anywhere else."

"How do you know, my dear? You've never been anywhere else."

Soon it was decided. Clara would go to boarding school in the spring.

Clara felt sad at the new school. She missed home. The more she tried to like the new school, the lonelier she became.

"Clara," her teacher said one day, "today's lesson is about the kings who ruled ancient Egypt."

"Yes, sir."

"These kings made up a dynasty or line of royalty. Do you recall the name of this dynasty?"

Clara knew the answer.

"Pot-lemy," she stated proudly.

A loud laugh came from the back of the room. "Did you hear what she said? Potlemy!"

Soon the entire class was laughing. The teacher beat the narrow rod he was holding. "Quiet!"

Clara realized she had made a mistake. She had given the right answer but pronounced it wrong. She buried her face in her hands.

The teacher walked to Clara and whispered that she could leave the room. Not stopping to gather her books, she ran out. She didn't stop until she reached her own room. Throwing herself on the bed, she cried herself to sleep.

CLARA REALIZED SHE MADE A MISTAKE.

CLARA BARTON

Several days later as she read a book, Clara heard soft tapping on the door.

"Come in," she called.

Her teacher opened the door and pulled up a chair next to the bed.

"Clara, you have visitors."

"Who?"

"Your father and brother. David, I believe."

"Oh, how wonderful. I can't wait to see them." She smiled brightly, but her teacher looked serious. "Is something wrong, sir?"

"We decided it would be best for you to go home. We know you haven't been eating or sleeping well."

Clara hung her head. "I'm sorry. I like school, but I miss home so much."

"I know," he answered. "Now, you'd better get yourself packed up. That brother of yours looked as if he didn't like to be kept waiting."

"Now I know it's David." Clara jumped off the bed and threw her arms around her teacher. "I will miss you," she whispered.

An hour later, the Barton carriage was rolling

26

"CLARA, YOU HAVE VISITORS."

homeward. Father held the reins as David told his sister of the move they had just made.

"You should see our new farm. Stephen and I found several arrowheads near the gate."

"A new farm! I can hardly wait to see it."

"But there's work to be done," Father said. "Your mother will need help."

"Oh, I want to help. It will be fun!" Clara was bursting with excitement.

There *was* work to do. The farmhouse needed a coat of paint and many repairs. Although the farm was large, the Barton "family" had grown, too. Father had taken in some relatives and a boy.

Often Clara would climb Rocky Hill, where she could look out over the countryside. She wondered what she would become when she grew up. She could never make up her mind.

Then an accident helped her decide.

A barn was being raised on the Barton farm. Men from miles around came to work. The women fixed food. Clara's mother placed her in charge of pouring milk.

THE FARMHOUSE NEEDED A COAT OF PAINT.

The morning passed quickly, and soon the men crowded in line for lunch. Clara poured glass after glass of milk.

At about three o'clock, Clara was finally able to sit down for a rest. She had just taken a sip of milk when she heard a loud scream. She ran toward the crowd.

"What happened?" No one answered. Clara pushed to the front of the crowd and looked up. Dangling from swaying ropes were two planks that had split in half. Directly below, men were helping a boy to his feet.

"David!" Clara rushed forward. "What happened to you?"

"Just. . .took a little tumble. Nothing to worry about."

David started to walk. He stumbled and was caught by two men.

"Are you all right, David?" Father stepped forward and examined his son's head. "That was quite a fall you took."

"I'm all right. Just let me rest a bit, and I'll be

"ARE YOU ALL RIGHT, DAVID?"

back on the job."

As the crowd broke up, Clara and Father helped David to a shady place.

"You're limping," Clara noticed.

"Now don't you worry about me, Clara. I could race you to the river and beat you by a mile. You go mind the milk stand."

Clara had forgotten all about the milk. Several people were waiting in line.

"All right, but you rest."

"Yes, Mother." David gave his sister a wink.

But David was not all right. That night his head throbbed, and the next day he had a fever. The Bartons sent for a doctor.

By the time the doctor arrived, David's moans filled the house.

"David is a very sick young man," the doctor told the Bartons. "I tried to give him medicine, but he refused to take it."

Mama gasped. "What can we do?"

"Doctor, may I try giving him the medicine?" Clara asked.

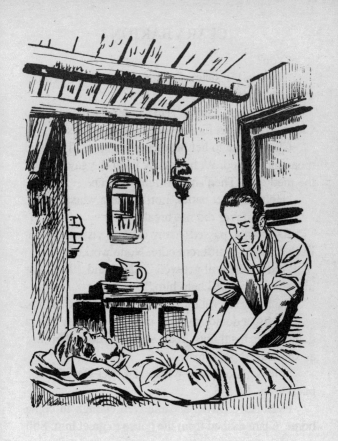

DAVID'S MOANS FILLED THE HOUSE.

CLARA BARTON

"You?"

"This is his sister, Doctor. She and her brother are very close."

"I guess you can try." He handed the medicine to Clara. "Try to get him to take two spoonfuls."

Clara spoke to her brother in whispers. The loud moaning quieted. With a steady hand she gave David the medicine. Then she left him to sleep.

"Help him get better, Lord," Clara whispered.

But the fever did not break.

As months passed, many doctors visited David. Each brought a different cure. None worked.

"I know he will get well," Clara said. "Just give him time. God will help him."

Each day she sat by David's bed and read to him.

Finally a doctor came to take David away. Clara gathered up his things. Tears streamed down her face as she waved good-bye.

"Please, God," she whispered, "let David come back to us. Please."

Eventually David became well enough to come home. Clara dashed from the house to greet him. Still

SHE SAT BY DAVID'S BED AND READ TO HIM.

pale, David hugged his sister with all his strength.

"Little one," he exclaimed, "you're the one who needs to become healthy. You're as tiny as a wart."

Together Clara and David regained their strength. Often they took the big family Bible and headed outside. Sitting in the shade, they shared the stories of Jesus.

"Just think," David said one afternoon, "Jesus could cure anyone."

"I love it when He brought Jairus's daughter back from the dead," Clara mused.

"You almost did that for me," David said. "I think you have a special talent for helping the sick."

Clara thought about David's words. Could the Lord mean for her to help sick people?

"Please give direction to my life," Clara prayed often. "And give me strength to do Your will."

THEY SHARED THE STORIES OF JESUS.

"YOU HAVE A VERY INTERESTING DAUGHTER."

3

Clara sat on the sofa, buried beneath a mound of blankets. "Mumps!" she muttered. "What a way to be sick." She hated being sick, especially with company in the house.

Clara could hear her parents talking with their guest Mr. Fowler, a famous lecturer. Suddenly she heard her name.

"You have a very interesting daughter in Miss Clara," Mr. Fowler said. "Her features show great strength."

"True, Mr. Fowler," agreed Mama. "But she is so shy. She loves people, yet is timid with them."

"Give her some responsibilities. She would be a perfect teacher."

The Bartons wasted no time in taking his advice. Soon it was arranged for Clara to teach in the nearby District 9 schoolhouse.

On a crisp spring morning, fifteen-year-old Clara marched up the pathway to her new school. She opened the door of the one-room building and was greeted by a loud chorus.

"Good morning, Miss Barton."

Before her were forty faces. Making her way between the wooden benches, Clara walked to the teacher's desk. Picking up a Bible, she announced that the class would read a few verses.

As the children read, Clara felt wonderful. Her students wanted to learn, and she would guide them.

When recess came, the children scrambled outside. Then trouble arrived.

"Miss Barton! The big boys won't let us play with our ball," cried a little girl, her clothes covered with dust.

"Doesn't every grade have a ball?"

"GOOD MORNING, MISS BARTON."

"Yes, Miss Barton. But the boys take them. When I tried to get ours back, they pushed me."

Clara strode out to the playground. Four tall boys held the balls.

"I understand we have a problem. These balls must be shared."

"There ain't no misunderstandin', Teacher. We're sharin'. See? Bill's got two, George's got three, Henry's got—"

"Each grade is to have one ball. Now why don't you boys—"

"Teacher, why don't you let us get back to our game." Turning his back, the boy heaved a ball toward a barrel forty yards away. The ball fell about two feet short.

"What's the matter? Can't you throw that far?" Clara asked.

The boy flashed her an angry look, then threw again. The ball passed the barrel by several feet.

"Too bad! You should practice more."

"All right, Teacher. Show me how." The boy tossed a ball to Clara.

"WHAT'S THE MATTER?
CAN'T YOU THROW THAT FAR?"

Clara knew she had to hit her target. "Lord, help me," she prayed. Blocking the sun with her free hand, she thrust the ball straight ahead.

All eyes watched the ball whiz through the air. It dropped into the barrel. The small children erupted in cheers.

Clara turned to the four boys. "Shall we return to the classroom? We might find something for you to read on the subject of throwing–and something else on the subject of manners."

She turned and marched triumphantly to the school. "Thank You, Lord," she whispered.

In the months that followed, Clara became known as a good teacher. The older boys admired her for her strength and agility. The younger children loved to hear her stories.

On the final day, Clara thanked her students for their help. As they left, each child handed her a small present. When the schoolhouse was empty, Clara noticed an envelope on top of the gifts. Opening it, she found a slightly smudged sign: *To the Champion Teacher.*

ALL EYES WATCHED THE BALL
WHIZ THROUGH THE AIR.

She looked toward the door and saw four smiling boys peeking in.

Teaching gave Clara confidence. Job offers flowed in. For once, new places did not frighten her.

While Clara taught, David and Stephen became owners of several lumber factories. During the summer, Clara helped them. She suggested forming a school for children of the factory workers.

"They need a school," she pleaded. "Can't you find me a patch of space for a classroom?"

Stephen and David offered her an unused packing room. The first day of school brought seventy children, one tame crow, and two pet goats. Clara persuaded her brothers to build a real school. Soon there were 125 children.

For ten years, Clara taught. Finally Clara decided *she* ought to go back to school.

In 1850, Clara entered the Liberal Institute in Clinton, New York. She became close friends with another student, Mary Norton.

After graduating, Clara paid Mary a visit in New Jersey. The Nortons treated Clara as one of the

THE FIRST DAY OF SCHOOL
BROUGHT SEVENTY CHILDREN.

family, and she enjoyed herself. But one thing bothered her.

"Mary, why are children roaming the streets?" As the two women shopped, they were constantly shoved by young boys.

"Why don't you ask one of them?" Mary answered.

"I will." Clara caught the collar of one of the boys running by. "Why aren't you in school?" she asked.

"Who's got money for school, lady?" The boy darted away.

"What did he mean by that, Mary?"

"Well, Bordentown schools are private. You have to pay to attend. We don't have schools that are open for everyone."

"Well, it's time you did have open schools. Whom can I talk to about this matter?"

"Mr. Suydam is head of the school board," Mary said.

"Where is he?"

"About two doorways straight ahead. He's the postmaster, too."

"WHY AREN'T YOU IN SCHOOL?"

Clara sped toward the post office. Behind the counter stood a bearded man.

"May I help you ladies?"

"Yes, you may," Clara said. "And you might also help the young people in this town."

The old man was startled. Few women spoke so forcefully.

"I want to know why children are running all over the streets of this town," Clara continued. "I want to know why they aren't in school. I want to know why–"

"Please! I don't know your name, young lady, but–"

"My name isn't important, but my questions are. You are the head of the school board?"

The man nodded.

"Are you aware that a New Jersey law says each child must receive a free education?"

"Yes, but we have several private schools in the area which take care–"

"Of those students who can afford to go. Isn't that correct?"

"MAY I HELP YOU, LADIES?"

"Well, there is a tuition fee, though I don't see–"

"Then a New Jersey law is not being enforced in this town."

"But no one has ever suggested we have free school. All the people–"

"It has now been suggested! How many youngsters attend your private schools?"

"About two hundred–eight more than last year." Mr. Suydam beamed in pride.

"And how many youngsters in this town are *not* attending school?"

"I, well, I. . .guess there might be about four hundred."

"Those figures show that a new school is needed. I offer my services as a teacher."

"But the school budget doesn't call for–"

"There is no need for a salary at this point, Mr. Suydam. May I count on your help?"

The man was stunned. "I suppose–"

"Good, we'll start making plans immediately." Clara turned and marched out the door.

She got her school. In three years, attendance

"I OFFER MY SERVICES AS A TEACHER."

rose from six to six hundred. Eventually Clara's health gave way. She lost her voice completely, and her doctors ordered her to take a long rest.

Returning home from town one afternoon, Clara overheard a group of people talking.

"It sure doesn't look good in Washington. I hate to think what's going to happen," a man said.

"Sure looks like a war's shapin' up," another grumbled.

Clara could not sleep that night. She tossed and turned. She prayed. Suddenly she sat up and lit a candle.

"I'm going to Washington!" she announced. "I might be needed there."

"I'M GOING TO WASHINGTON."

WASHINGTON WAS AN EXCITING CITY.

4

Clara stood before the mirror and smoothed her dress. This was her first day at a new job.

On top of her bureau lay a letter from Congressman Alexander DeWitt, a family friend. When she'd decided to go to Washington, Clara had written Mr. DeWitt. He found Clara a job with the United States Patent Office.

Clara gave her room one last look. Stuffing a lace handkerchief into her handbag, she closed and locked the door.

Washington was an exciting city. More than forty thousand people lived in the nation's capital.

CLARA BARTON

Visitors streamed into the city from all over the world.

Yet there was a strange feeling. Men huddled together and spoke in whispers. Clara wondered if they were discussing war.

Clara was not welcomed by everyone when she arrived at the patent office. Some men blew smoke in her face. A few spit tobacco juice at her feet.

Mr. Mason, the man who had hired Clara, met her with a smile. He asked her into his office. She seated herself in an overstuffed chair.

"Mr. Mason, many of your workers are not happy about my presence here."

"Well, Miss Barton, I'm afraid that some of our men will not treat you pleasantly."

"Have I done something to offend them?"

"Of course not. But you are the first woman clerk in Washington. Men have always held clerks' jobs."

"It seems to me that a position should be held by the person who can do it best."

"My feelings as well, Miss Barton. But some

"MEN HAVE ALWAYS HELD CLERKS' JOBS."

people disagree. You will probably receive some rude treatment for a while."

"I appreciate your help, Mr. Mason." Clara stood. "Now, may I see where I am to work? I had best start proving my worth."

"Certainly, Miss Barton."

Clara was led to a large table piled with books and papers. It was difficult to ignore the sneers of the clerks, but Clara reminded herself of Jesus' words: *Love your enemies*.

"You will copy the information on these records into these books," Mr. Mason explained. "Mr. DeWitt said your writing is very neat. You'll certainly be able to display your talent here." Mr. Mason smiled and excused himself.

Clara's job was tiring. Her fingers grew sore, and her back ached. She missed her family and friends. Sometimes Clara spent her free time listening to speeches in the United States Senate.

"Each state should decide for itself whether slavery is legal," declared southern senators.

Northern senators disagreed.

"EACH STATE SHOULD DECIDE
WHETHER SLAVERY IS LEGAL."

CLARA BARTON

When President James Buchanan was elected in 1856 to replace President Pierce, Clara lost her job and went home to Massachusetts. Soon she received a letter from the patent office.

"We have been unable to secure a competent replacement for you," the letter read. "Please consider returning."

Clara traveled back to Washington. She found an uneasy city. Crowds gathered at street corners. Angry speakers shouted at people walking by.

In November 1860, Abraham Lincoln was elected president. Immediately seven southern states agreed to withdraw from the United States. They elected their own president.

In Washington, Clara received an invitation to attend the Inaugural Ball in honor of President Lincoln. The morning of March 4, 1861, was brisk. Clara bundled herself well and walked to the Capitol. She listened to Abraham Lincoln take the oath of office. After his speech, Clara hurried home. By afternoon, she was sick.

"I will be unable to attend the ball," she wrote to

IN NOVEMBER 1860,
LINCOLN WAS ELECTED PRESIDENT.

a friend that night. "It is a sad disappointment to me. But I only pray that President Lincoln can find a way to pull the country together. The talk of war is everywhere. Voices are loud and angry. I am reminded of an old saying from Proverbs–'A soft answer turneth away wrath.' There seem to be no soft answers anymore, only bitter and noisy argument. Surely our actions cannot please God."

THE TALK OF WAR WAS EVERYWHERE.

"HEY, THERE'S MISS BARTON."

5

"The South opened fire on Fort Sumter."

Clara could not believe her ears as she hurried to work one April morning in 1861.

Soon young soldiers flooded the city.

One day Clara stood on the platform at the Washington train station. In a few minutes, a train would steam in bearing soldiers from her hometown in Massachusetts.

As the train pulled in, Clara smiled and waved.

"Hey, there's Miss Barton!" a voice shouted.

Soon Clara was surrounded by friends and former students.

In the weeks that followed, Clara made frequent trips to the Capitol to visit the soldiers. The Massachusetts regiments were housed in the Senate chambers. Clara tore up sheets and wrapped them into rolls of bandages for the soldiers. She sewed up ragged uniforms. Sometimes she baked delicious pies.

Wounded soldiers were brought to the Capitol lawn because there was no better place to take them. As Clara walked to the Senate chambers one morning, she noticed a soldier sleeping on the lawn. A large wound on his head looked badly infected. Clara strode to one of the doctors nearby.

"Sir, I believe you have a patient with a severe wound that has not been attended to. Do you suppose—"

"Do *you* suppose you might just go about your own business and leave us alone?" the doctor snapped.

"But this boy's wound is infected. He needs help right away. If he—"

"They all need help right away. Now, if you don't mind, I have other things to do."

WOUNDED SOLDIERS WERE BROUGHT
TO THE CAPITOL LAWN.

"But I do mind!" Clara said. "If that boy had received proper treatment, he would not be in the condition he is in now."

"If he had received proper treatment at the battlefield, he would probably be recovered by now."

"Then why didn't he?" Clara asked.

"No one is there. Now if you will excuse me, I have several things to take care of."

The doctor walked away, leaving Clara gazing at hundreds of wounded soldiers.

"Someone *should* be there when these boys are shot. I'm going to find out why they aren't."

CLARA GAZED AT THE WOUNDED SOLDIERS.

A MAN WAS CARRYING THE CANDLE.

6

The supply wagon came to a jerky halt as Clara tugged on the reins. It was almost midnight, and she had been traveling since daybreak.

Clara stepped down from the wagon and looked around. No one was nearby. Wearily she climbed the stairs to a building and entered.

Once inside, Clara could hear the moans of wounded men. A candle moved. Clara walked toward it, being careful not to fall over any of the injured soldiers on the floor.

A man was carrying the candle. His doctor's jacket was dirty.

"Sir. . .sir."

The doctor turned. "What are you doing here?" He was not happy.

"I've come to help."

"You've come to help! And what can you do? Sweep the floor?" He turned abruptly and moved to another soldier.

Clara turned to leave, but then she stopped. Hadn't she worked for days collecting supplies? Weren't there hundreds of men in this room who needed help? *I need Your strength,* Clara prayed.

She walked back to the doctor. "I have come a long way to help," she said quietly. "I have things in my wagon which I think you can use."

"And what are these things? Cookies? Cakes? Young lady, I'm sure you mean well by coming here, but I'm afraid–"

"I am not speaking of cookies," Clara interrupted. "I am speaking of medicine, bandages, shirts, socks."

"Are you telling the truth?"

"If you follow me, you will see that I am." Clara marched outside. The doctor followed eagerly. He

"ARE YOU TELLING THE TRUTH?"

climbed into the wagon.

"I can't believe it. How did you get these things? Who are you? Where did you come from?"

"Later on we can talk. Right now we had best unload these things."

"Yes, yes!"

The two worked through the night.

"Some of these things should be taken into Culpepper," the doctor said the next morning. "I'll get a man to take them."

"I'll do it. I'm the only one who knows what things are in which boxes."

"But you're tired. Don't you wish to rest?" the doctor asked.

"That will come later. May I go?"

"Well, if you wish, miss. Say, I don't even know your name."

"Miss Barton, sir. Clara Barton."

"And I am Dr. Dunne. James Dunne. I'm pleased to meet you, Miss Barton. And I apologize for my lack of manners earlier."

"That's quite all right, sir. Now, may I go?"

"MISS BARTON , SIR. CLARA BARTON."

"Certainly."

Clara and Dr. Dunne loaded several boxes of medicine and clothing back into the wagon. Soon Clara was headed down the road.

The tiny town of Culpepper lay in ruins. Clara stopped her wagon. "Could you tell me where I might find the military hospital?" she asked a man.

"You mean hospitals, don't you, miss? Any of these buildings."

"All these buildings are hospitals?" Clara's voice showed her surprise.

"Yup. There's Yankees and Rebs in every one."

Shocked, Clara climbed down and entered the nearest building. Everywhere she looked there were injured soldiers.

Wasting no time, Clara began unloading supplies. She was soon helped by several doctors. Word spread through the hospital of her arrival. Soldiers greeted her joyfully.

The next few weeks were busy. Clara applied new bandages, gave medicine, cooked meals, and wrote letters for the men.

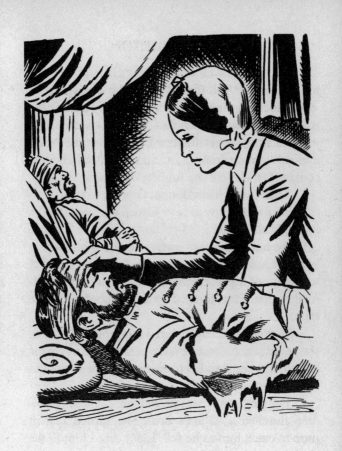

SHE APPLIED BANDAGES.

CLARA BARTON

One day bad news arrived. "General Jackson has attacked at Bull Run. Sounds like a slaughter."

A doctor arranged for Clara to go by train to the battlefield. Loading supplies into a boxcar, Clara stopped to wipe her forehead. Suddenly she heard a chant coming from the Culpepper hospitals. She could just make out the soldiers' words.

"Thank you, Miss Barton. God bless you."

Clara was happy to have helped the men. But the job had just begun.

The train ride was bumpy. Clara did her best to keep the stacks of supplies from falling over. After traveling all night, the train pulled into a tiny railroad station. Clara jumped up and climbed out of the train.

Wounded soldiers covered the ground as far as she could see. A chain of wagons stretched along the road to the horizon. Each wagon was crowded with soldiers moaning in pain.

"Begging your pardon, ma'am." A young soldier clutched at Clara's arm. She turned just in time to catch him as he fell. Clara eased him to the

GENERAL JACKSON'S ARMY ATTACKED AT BULL RUN.

ground. He had been shot in the chest.

"Ma'am, are you Miss Barton?"

"Yes, son. Now lie quietly, and we'll take care of you." Clara wiped the boy's head with her apron. "Quickly," she called to a nearby soldier, "bring me that small brown bag from the boxcar."

"I'm afraid it's too late for that, Miss Barton. But would you do me a favor? My name's Harvey Johnstone. Would you tell my folks good-bye? They're staying just outside Washington with some people named Clarke. I'd be greatly indebted to you if–"

The boy died in Clara's arms. Her eyes filled with tears.

"Here's your bag, ma'am."

Clara took the bag from the soldier. Pulling a piece of paper from it, she scribbled down the boy's name and wrote the name Clarke beside it. Then she shoved it back into the bag.

"Miss Barton, should we start unloading?"

"Yes, of course. From the look of things, I'd say these men need food."

In minutes, Clara was cooking huge kettles of

"ARE YOU MISS BARTON?"

stew. The smell of food brought smiles to many soldiers.

Next, Clara tried to make the wounded more comfortable. Bales of hay were scattered on the ground to make softer beds.

Then Clara began cleaning and dressing wounds. When evening arrived, it grew cold. She worried about men getting pneumonia. She walked up and down rows of the injured, making sure they were covered with quilts or blankets.

As she knelt beside one man, she noticed a light growing larger several yards away. A small fire had started from a candle being tipped over. She threw down the nearest quilt and smothered the fire.

For the rest of the night, Clara watched for fires.

Dawn was a welcome sight. Clara busied herself boiling hot coffee.

Suddenly a Union scout raced into camp.

"They're coming. The Confederate cavalry. They're just over that hill."

A chill raced through Clara. How could the hundreds of wounded men be moved?

A UNION SCOUT RACED INTO CAMP.

Soon the wagons were being loaded with the injured. Clara made sure each wagon had some food.

"Miss Barton, you'd best leave this area. The danger is very great." A Union officer looked worried as he spoke.

"I can't leave now. There are men to be cared for."

"But you may be captured, Miss Barton."

"And you might be, too, sir. But you are not leaving."

"These are my men. It's my job to see that they are kept safe."

"Then I suggest we load them faster." Clara flashed a smile.

By midafternoon, heavy drizzle covered the area. Men were being loaded onto trains. Cannon fire came closer.

Finally all the injured were loaded. Clara was pulled into a boxcar. She took a final look at the muddy scene.

As the train chugged its way down the tracks, a soldier shouted that Confederates were attacking the camp. Clara stared sadly out into the night.

THE TRAIN CHUGGED ITS WAY DOWN THE TRACKS.

THE ARMY WAGON SURGED FORWARD.

7

"Miss Barton, let me help you."

A huge Union soldier helped Clara up into an army wagon.

"Thank you. I'm afraid I wouldn't have been able to make it myself."

"From what I hear, you're able to do just about everything. Giddyap, you long-eared mulies!"

The army wagon surged forward on the Washington road. The driver often waved to people.

"Do you know all those people you're waving at?" Clara asked.

"Nope, but its kinda fun to pretend."

Clara smiled. She was going to like her new driver. "Can the wagon move any faster?" she asked.

"Sure can, Miss Barton. Hold on." The driver snapped the whip above the mules' heads, and the wagon rolled rapidly out of the city.

"How far is it to Harpers Ferry?"

" 'Bout eighty miles, Miss Barton. But this road will make it seem like eight hundred. More bumps on it than on a toad's back."

The wagon bounced all over the road, but Pete drove with a careful hand.

"I hear that battle at Chantilly was a terrible mess," Pete said. "Heard you almost got caught by those Rebs."

Clara nodded. Chantilly had been terrible. General Lee sent his troops to destroy the small town in Virginia. By the time Clara had arrived, the town was ruined. Hundreds lay injured. When the Confederates swooped down for a final attack, she'd escaped on horseback.

"Say, look up ahead!" Pete slowed the horses.

Hundreds of wagons crawled along the road as

GENERAL LEE SENT HIS TROOPS
TO DESTROY THE SMALL TOWN.

far as they could see.

"Isn't there something we can do, Pete? We will never get to Harpers Ferry behind this mess."

"Nuthin' much we can do, Miss Barton. The road's too narrow for passing. Looks like those wagons up front are pullin' off for the night. Guess we might as well, too."

The wagon creaked to the side of the road. Clara climbed down and began cooking supper.

After eating, Clara took a walk. Wounded soldiers were scattered by the road. She helped whenever she could. Suddenly she had an idea. Hurrying back to the wagon, she jostled Pete out of his sleep.

"Pete, we can go now!"

Pete rolled over and sat up.

"Who. . .what. . .what's happened?" he asked.

"It's time to go," Clara exclaimed. "Look! The moon is full, and the road is bare. We can travel tonight and pass all these wagons."

Pete was finally awake. He stared at Clara.

"But we need rest. Now why don't you crawl into the wagon and get–"

WOUNDED SOLDIERS WERE SCATTERED BY THE ROAD.

CLARA BARTON

Clara stared at him. "If you won't drive this wagon, I will."

Pete scratched his head. "Well, my orders are to take you where you want to go. I guess that means when, too."

Clara quickly loaded the things they had used for cooking. Pete lined up the mules, and soon the lonely wagon was rolling over the road. The next morning, it had passed hundreds of wagons and was near the head of the train.

By noon, Clara was in Harpers Ferry. She quickly took charge of the injured.

The next morning, excitement filled Harpers Ferry. News had drifted in that Confederate and Union troops were preparing to clash about ten miles away.

"The battle will take place on Antietam Creek. That's right near Sharpsburg, Maryland." The soldier spreading the news was shaking. "Generals Lee and Jackson are lining up their soldiers. Gonna fight McClellan, Burnside, and Hooker. What a battle!"

In no time, Clara loaded a wagon. By afternoon,

PETE LINED UP THE MULES.

she was at a farmhouse-hospital. Cannons exploded nearby. As Clara jumped down from the wagon, a welcome face greeted her.

"Dr. Dunne, how good to see you again!"

"And how wonderful to see you, Clara. I've heard so much about you since our first meeting. We must have a long talk."

"Yes, but let's get my wagon unloaded."

"I won't ask if you brought cookies." Dr. Dunne's eyes twinkled.

Clara and Dr. Dunne worked long hours. The farmhouse was flooded with injured soldiers.

"I don't understand this war," Dr. Dunne burst out one day. "Some of these boys are fighting members of their own family."

Clara knelt to give a Union soldier a drink of water. She, too, could not understand the war.

Crack! A bullet tore through the sleeve of Clara's dress. The bullet hit the soldier. He lay dead.

After a moment, Clara stood up and walked to the next injured man. The living had to be helped.

As the battle at Antietam went on, cannon fire

CLARA GAVE A UNION SOLDIER A DRINK OF WATER.

came closer to the farmhouse. At times, everything would shake. Finally came the news Clara had feared.

"Miss Barton, there's no food. What'll we do?"

Clara tried to think of something. "How about the medicine we brought along to treat snakebite? What's it packed in?"

"I'll go see."

The soldier disappeared into the cellar. He soon returned with three wooden cases. He pried them open and began uncovering the bottles of medicine.

"Hallelujah!" he exclaimed.

Clara came running. "What is it?"

"Look, Miss Barton!"

Clara took a handful of soft yellow powder from one of the cases. "Cornmeal!"

"Miss Barton, it's like a miracle!"

"Well, let's use this miracle. Get a fire set up outside. We'll make the biggest batch of cornmeal gruel you've ever seen. Somebody go down into the cellar and see if there are any kettles."

Two soldiers sprang to their feet and ran down the cellar stairs. "Miss Barton! Come down here!"

"CORNMEAL!"

Clara hurried into the cellar.

"Look, Miss Barton. Three bags of flour and a whole bag of salt. Must have been stored here for years. Can we use 'em?"

"Of course. We'll make hardtack. These men will have a feast."

Soon the huge kitchen ovens were filled with hardtack bread. In the yard, a giant kettle bubbled with cornmeal gruel. Clara ran from oven to kettle, making sure nothing burned.

That evening after hundreds of men had been fed warm meals, Clara sat down. A cheerful harmonica began playing.

"Now I know how the Lord's disciples felt."

Clara glanced up to find Dr. Dunne nearby.

"Beg pardon, Doctor?" Clara said.

"Remember the loaves and fishes, Miss Barton? How the Lord fed thousands with a few loaves of bread and a couple of fish?"

Clara nodded. "We're told the Lord works in mysterious ways," she answered. "I think He provided this food just for our men."

A CHEERFUL HARMONICA BEGAN PLAYING.

"HOW DO YOU DO SO MUCH WITH SO LITTLE?"

8

"Miss Barton, I have one question."

Clara could hardly speak. The quartermaster general had been reading her report of what had happened at Antietam.

"Yes, sir."

"How do you do so much with so little?"

"Dr. Dunne is the one who deserves your praise, General Rucker. I only wish he–"

"I have the highest regard for Dr. Dunne. But you, Miss Barton, you are a woman. It is hard to believe you could stand up under all this. I understand that you recently received an honor from the men of the

Twenty-first Massachusetts Regiment. Is that true?"

"Why, yes. How did you know?"

"Top secret, Miss Barton." The general winked. "You are far more famous than you realize."

"General Rucker, I'm not interested in being famous. I'm interested in this report. We lost so many lives. Isn't there any hope of this war ending?"

"Miss Barton, there is always hope."

Clara rose from her seat. She walked to the window. "It's so sad to see young boys going to war. Many never go home."

She returned to the desk. "Where may I go that I will be most needed?"

General Rucker pulled out a map. He pointed to a small dot by a crooked line.

"This is Fredericksburg, and this is the Rappahannock River. There's a deserted mansion called the Lacy House right about here."

"I shall leave in the morning." Clara tied her bonnet and walked to the door. "Oh, General Rucker, may I have three wagons for this trip? The last time–"

"No, you may not have three wagons!" General

"MISS BARTON, THERE IS ALWAYS HOPE."

Rucker's eyes twinkled. "You shall have six wagons and an ambulance."

"Thank you," Clara whispered.

The Lacy mansion, with its twelve rooms, stood empty under a heavy blanket of snow. Clara shivered as she carried her lantern through the lonely house. Each room was ready for the task ahead.

Walking out to the patio, Clara looked down the hill. Below her lay the river. Nearby, Union campfires glowed. Across the river, the Confederates held Fredericksburg. There was no bridge. The Union soldiers would build one. It would not be easy.

Early the next morning, Clara awakened to the shouts of men. Rushing to her window, she saw Union soldiers working on a bridge. By afternoon, the first attack was under way.

A cannon bellowed from the opposite shore. Soldiers crossing the bridge were thrown into the water and carried downstream.

More cannons blasted. The Lacy mansion shook from the explosions. The front door flew open.

"Here come the injured!" a lieutenant called.

A CANNON BELLOWED FROM THE OPPOSITE SHORE.

Clara raced to the door. Stretcher after stretcher was being carried up the yard.

The rooms were soon packed with Union soldiers. They were on the staircase, in the cellar–anyplace they might be safe.

"Our men are in Fredericksburg!" The news roared through the house. Clara looked out the window and could see a line of blue uniforms crossing the bridge.

A redheaded boy ran up to her. He stuffed a note into her hand: *Come to me. Your place is here.*

"Where did you come from?" she asked the boy.

"Fredericksburg. The doctor there said to get you."

"I'll have to gather supplies. Here, keep this bag open and follow me." Clara stuffed the bag with medicine.

One of the doctors tried to stop her. "You can't make it over that bridge. We've already lost hundreds of soldiers."

Clara wouldn't listen. Scrambling over the bridge, she heard a shot whistle past. It seemed to take hours to get across. Reaching the opposite shore, Clara

STRETCHER AFTER STRETCHER WAS BEING CARRIED.

stumbled up the hill. The boy caught up with her and led her into Fredericksburg.

A Union officer rode up. "You're in great danger, ma'am. Do you want protection?" he asked.

"Thank you, General. But I believe I'm the best-protected woman in the country. I have the entire army as my guard."

Some soldiers overheard her. They cheered wildly. "Hooray for the Union! Hooray for Miss Barton!"

The general smiled down. "Ma'am, I believe you are right."

Clara entered a shattered wooden building filled with injured men.

"Clara! Clara Barton!"

"Dr. Cutter!" Clara went up to the old surgeon.

"I knew you'd come, Clara. I hated to call on you, but we need you so badly."

Clara smiled at the doctor. He was a member of the Massachusetts Twenty-first Regiment. *Her* regiment.

"Clara, we have our hands full. The wounded keep pouring in. We'll have to get them back across

"I KNEW YOU'D COME, CLARA."

the river. I heard you have the old Lacy mansion."

"Yes, it was filling fast when I left. But if these boys must be moved, we will find room for them."

Clara and Dr. Cutter started moving the injured. Soon Lacy House bulged with twelve hundred wounded men. They shivered in the cold December air. But each face lit up as the tiny woman they knew and loved came near.

Christmas night, as Clara stared out her window, a light snow began falling. She thought of Christmases in the little farmhouse in Oxford. She thought of her family.

Loud singing broke out. Clara flung open her door. She stood speechless as a crowd of men sang: "Happy birthday, Miss Barton. Happy birthday to you."

"How did you know?"

The only answer she received was the smiling faces of her patients.

When the injured had been cared for, Clara went back to Washington for more supplies. She pulled her cape close as she stepped off the streetcar near her home.

"HAPPY BIRTHDAY, MISS BARTON."

CLARA BARTON

Clara unlocked the door of her room and stumbled in. Lighting a candle, she noticed a box on her bed. Her name was written on it.

Clara cut through the cord around the box. A small card fell to the floor. Clara picked it up. *From your friends in Oxford and Worcester,* she read.

Clara was amazed. The box was full of shoes, gloves, shirts, collars, and a dress! She held up the lovely green silk and whirled around the room. Her tired body came alive.

In a few weeks, Clara had a chance to show off her new dress. She received a note to go to Ward 17 of Lincoln Hospital.

Why do they want me there? she wondered. She put on her new dress and hurried off.

As she walked through the door, a great cheer arose. Before her stood seventy men, injured soldiers from the Battle of Fredericksburg. They saluted her.

"I don't know what to say," she gasped. "It's all so wonderful!"

"And so are you, Miss Barton!" the men shouted. "You're the best soldier in the country!"

A GREAT CHEER AROSE.

A KITTEN TANGLED ITSELF IN
LONG STRANDS OF YARN.

9

A kitten tangled itself in long strands of yarn. Clara looked down from her darning and chuckled.

"Now see what you've done. How will we ever get you loose?" She lifted the kitten into her lap and pulled the yarn away.

"I shall miss you while I'm gone." The kitten had been a present from the Speaker of the House of Representatives, Schuyler Colfax. But there was no place for a tiny pet on the battlefront. Clara was preparing to leave Washington for South Carolina. The Union Navy was going to attack Charleston.

By afternoon, supplies were loaded on the *Aragon,* a small transport ship. Clara took her kitten to a neighbor. Soon she was sailing toward the wooded hills of the Carolinas.

Clara had become known as the angel of the battlefield, and soldiers cheered as she entered the harbor.

"I don't deserve this praise," she protested. "Many others have done far more than I." Nothing she said could stop the cheers.

Before long, Clara was in action. Union ships bombarded the Charleston harbor. Ship after ship returned, filled with wounded soldiers.

Clara moved the place for treatment to the islands outside Charleston. Now she could take care of the wounded more quickly.

The summer of 1863 brought new troubles. Whirling sand covered food and medicine. Insects attacked supplies. A scorching heat wave brought deadly fever.

"I must order you to go," Clara was told. "You are pale and look tired. I cannot risk having you stay. You

SUPPLIES WERE LOADED ON THE *ARAGON*.

should probably be in one of your own hospital beds."

"I'm all right," Clara insisted, and she stayed.

But Clara was wrong. In October, she collapsed. She lay in bed for weeks, unable to move. One day, she awoke to find a welcome visitor.

"David, is it really you?"

"Yes, Clara. It's your old brother, David."

Clara smiled. "Oh, David. I have to get out of this foolish bed. There's so much to do."

"Now listen, little one. The only thing that needs to be done right now is for you to get better. You came very near leaving us. It's time you rested."

"But David, what of the war? The soldiers?"

"And what of you? If you will not think of yourself, I shall have to. *You* are going to take a rest."

Clara followed her brother's orders. She boarded the *Aragon* and headed for Washington. From there she returned to Oxford and spent several weeks visiting friends. But the memories of injured soldiers drew her back to the battlefield. "Lord, give me the strength I need," she prayed.

The call came from Fredericksburg. Thousands

"DAVID—IS IT REALLY YOU?"

of soldiers lay injured. More than two thousand were dead.

Rain poured over Washington as Clara boarded a steamer early in May 1864. The crowded boat would take her down the Potomac. From Belle Plain Landing, she would go ten miles by wagon to Fredericksburg.

"Better get inside and find yourself a seat, lady," a deckhand called to her.

"Thank you," Clara answered. "Do you think this rain will stop soon?"

"Nope, and it's likely to be an awful muddy mess at Belle Plain."

He was right. As the boat steamed into the dock, Clara saw wagons stuck in mounds of mud.

"See what I mean?" the deckhand asked Clara. "Those wagons are full of our boys. Just no way to get 'em aboard."

"There has to be a way!" Clara snapped. She picked up her baskets and walked down the plank to the shore. She sank to her knees in mud.

"Can I help you, ma'am?" A young man offered

THE BOAT STEAMED INTO THE DOCK.

his hand to Clara, and she took it gratefully.

"I'm afraid the men in the wagons need your help more than I," she said

"We're doin' all we can for them. Are you from the Christian Commission?"

"No, but I'd be glad to help you if I can," Clara replied.

"We'd like to get these men fed. We've got some food–mostly crackers–and if we can find a place to heat some coffee. . ."

"There's a place." Clara rushed forward. "By that stump over there. See if you can gather up some brushwood. I'll get some kettles ready."

The kettles soon sizzled with boiling coffee.

"The men will be glad to get this," Clara's new friend said. "I only wish we had a way to take these crackers to them." He pointed to a large barrel.

"We can manage it quite easily." Clara pulled two linen scarves from her baskets. She flipped them open in the air. "Turn around," she ordered.

As the man turned, Clara tied one of the scarves around his waist.

THE KETTLES SOON SIZZLED WITH BOILING COFFEE.

"Never had an apron on before," he muttered.

"Well, this is a good time for it. Put some crackers onto your lap and fold the apron over them. Then tie it in, like this." Clara demonstrated with her own scarf.

"Say, that's clever. Have you been at any other battles?" the man asked.

"A few. Have you?"

"No, this is my first. I signed up for the Christian Commission. Want to do my part. Sure glad you came along."

"You'd have done all right," Clara said.

"Well, I'd best get some of this coffee delivered –and the crackers, too." He patted his apron and climbed into one of the wagons.

Fredericksburg was a skeleton of the city it had been. The few buildings that were not completely burned out served as hospitals. Wounded soldiers lay under trees, on wooden sidewalks, under wagons. Ambulances stood idle. Untreated men lay dying.

"Why aren't these men being treated?" Clara demanded. "Who is in charge?"

FREDERICKSBURG WAS A SKELETON OF
THE CITY IT HAD BEEN.

Clara's questions were met by blank looks. Men were dying, yet no one seemed to care. There was only one thing to do.

Getting a wagon, Clara raced back to Belle Plain. She boarded a steamer for Washington. That night, she was pounding on the door of Henry Wilson, chairman of the Senate's Military Committee.

"Senator, something must be done at Fredericksburg. Men are dying for lack of treatment, supplies, and medicine. Can't you do something?"

"Of course I can, Miss Barton!"

By ten o'clock that evening the quartermaster general and his staff climbed aboard a waiting steamer. The next day, order was returning to Fredericksburg. The city was a new place when Clara returned three days later. Every soldier was being treated.

"We owe you everything," one captain told Clara. "You've saved so many lives."

Clara shook her head. "It is God we must thank," she murmured. "Remember Psalm 46:1: 'God is our refuge and strength, a very present help in trouble.' Let us pray that this trouble will end soon."

"IT IS GOD WE MUST THANK."

LINCOLN WAS AGAIN SWORN IN AS PRESIDENT.

10

In March 1865, Abraham Lincoln was again sworn in as president. With the war drawing to a close, Clara had a new project in mind. She took her idea to Henry Wilson.

"Senator, these letters are from people all over the United States." Clara dumped two large bundles onto the senator's desk. "They have been addressed to me, I suppose, because of my connection with the war. Each letter asks a question. 'Where is my brother?' 'Have you heard of my son?' 'Can you help me find news of my husband?' Senator, I cannot answer these letters because I do not have the answers. But with the government's help, I think I could find them."

"Clara, the government has suffered a great expense from this war. You must–"

"I realize that many of these people have paid a very high price as well, Senator. Can you imagine the sadness these people feel? They want to know. They deserve to know."

Senator Wilson stared at the letters.

"You wish to undertake this job, Clara? Don't you feel you might use a rest?"

"Will these people be able to rest until they have their answers? Senator, this job needs to be done. I am willing to start right away, with your permission."

"This will take more than my permission. I will have to talk to the president."

President Lincoln was quick to agree with Clara. He sent her to Annapolis to set up a station.

On April 3, Robert E. Lee surrendered his troops to General Grant. The last cannon had sounded. The war was over. But on April 14, a final shot plunged

ROBERT E. LEE SURRENDERED HIS TROOPS.

the country into grief. President Lincoln had been killed.

In Annapolis, letters flooded the tent Clara was using. Records were checked and double-checked. Information drifted in. Clara made a list of missing men. She hoped to have it printed and distributed across the country. Then anyone with information about a missing person could contact her.

Printers told Clara that the list was too big to print. In desperation, she sent a letter to President Andrew Johnson. She prayed he would see the value of her work.

On the day he received Clara's letter, President Johnson sat down at his desk. He wrote: *Let this printing be done as speedily as possible, consistent with the public interest.*

With the lists of missing men printed, Clara arranged them according to states. She sent them to newspapers and hospitals. The response was quick.

Letters came from all over the country. Released prisoners, wounded men in hospitals, and officers scribbled down information. Often the listed men

SHE SENT A LETTER TO PRESIDENT JOHNSON.

were dead, but sometimes the men were in another part of the country. Pieces in the giant jigsaw puzzle slid into place. But one large piece was still missing.

"What happened to the soldiers at the Confederate prison in Andersonville?" Clara asked. "That prison in Georgia held thousands of captives."

The answer came from a surprising source.

"My name is Dorrence Atwater, Miss Barton. I believe I can help you."

Clara stared at the young man before her desk. His wrinkled face made him look old.

"How can you help us, Mr. Atwater? Please take a seat."

As the man collapsed into a chair, he handed a bundle of papers to Clara.

"I'm from Connecticut, Miss Barton. I enlisted when I was about sixteen. Those Rebs captured a bunch of us and took us to Andersonville. It was awful. They treated us like animals." The man's voice rose in anger.

"But how did you get these names?"

"A fever came along and started killin' off the

HIS WRINKLED FACE MADE HIM LOOK OLD.

prisoners. Killed some of the Confederates, too. I had it bad for a while, but somehow I got rid of it. When I got so I could see again, the guards put me into the surgeon's tent. Told me to keep a list for them of the dying. Each time a prisoner died, I had to write his name, date of death, and his regiment."

"Didn't the surgeon keep the list? How did you get this?"

"I made two lists. Tied one copy into my coat lining. Thought someone might want it someday. Read about you and what you were doin'. Thought you might be the one."

Clara leafed through the pages. There were thousands of names.

"Mr. Atwater, you have done a wonderful thing. You not only have done a great service for your country, but you will also answer the questions of thousands of families."

The man smiled. "I'm glad that I could do something to help out those fellows. That Andersonville prison was an awful place, Miss Barton."

"I know." Clara sighed. "One more thing, Mr.

"HOW DID YOU GET THIS?"

Atwater. Where were these men buried?"

"In the field at Andersonville. Guess there must be over ten thousand of 'em."

"And the graves, Mr. Atwater. Are they marked?"

"Nope. But that list has them recorded in the order they died, Miss Barton."

"Do you suppose if we went to Andersonville, you could help me put up markers for these men? I know you would probably hate to go back there, Mr. Atwater, but it would be so comforting to the families."

The man looked at the floor. Clara could understand his reluctance to go to the place where he had suffered so much.

"I see what you mean, Miss Barton. If you like, I'll go back with you."

Through the summer of 1865, Dorrence Atwater and Clara worked under a blazing sun. Each grave at Andersonville was marked. By fall, Clara had convinced Secretary of War Stanton to turn the Andersonville graveyard into a national cemetery.

Clara was anxious to get back to her work in

EACH GRAVE WAS MARKED.

Annapolis. When she returned, however, bad news waited.

"We're all out of money," one of the staff members announced.

Clara knew the government didn't have much money to give her. She had used her own savings, but that, too, was gone. Letters waited to be answered. More lists had to be distributed. The staff had to be paid.

"If only there were some way I could raise money," Clara said to a friend.

"You could talk," the friend suggested.

"What do you mean?"

"Clara, people would pay to hear you speak. You could tell them about the war, about your adventures."

"That's an idea. Perhaps I'd be able to locate more of our missing men."

It didn't take long to set up a series of lectures. The name "Clara Barton" appeared on signs in Indiana, Iowa, Illinois, Ohio, and Michigan. Old soldiers surrounded her to thank her for helping them.

OLD SOLDIERS SURROUNDED HER.

And after each lecture, Clara sent the money she received back to Annapolis.

By 1868, almost twenty-three thousand missing soldiers had been located. Clara closed the final record book at Annapolis and decided to continue lecturing.

But as she spoke in Portland, Maine, Clara lost her voice. Unable to continue, she walked off the stage.

"You need to rest, Clara," her doctor said. "You have been so busy with everyone else, you haven't been taking care of yourself. I suggest you take a rest for two or three years."

"But must I give up lecturing?"

"Of course. Why don't you go to Europe?"

Following her doctor's orders, Clara sailed for Europe in September 1869.

CLARA SAILED FOR EUROPE.

SHE WENT TO LONDON.

11

After a restful voyage, Clara unloaded her bags in Scotland. From there she went to London, then Paris, and finally to Geneva, Switzerland.

Throwing open her window one morning, Clara saw a carriage pull up. Several gentlemen stepped out and walked into the house.

Soon a knock came at her door.

"Miss Barton, there are some gentlemen to see you."

Clara went to meet her visitors.

"We're here as representatives of the International Convention of Geneva, Miss Barton," Dr. Appia said. "We've come to ask your country's help."

"I'm not sure I understand."

"Our organization has been trying to persuade the United States to join us in promoting the Red Cross."

"The Red Cross? I'm afraid I'm not familiar with the group."

"It's purpose is to help the wounded in war and people like yourself who are working in army hospitals. Any hospital flying this flag would be neutral and could not be captured."

Dr. Appia stood and unfurled a folded cloth. On a white background stood a deep red cross.

"It's beautiful, Dr. Appia," Clara exclaimed. "Your organization sounds interesting. It would be wonderful to have hospitals out of danger."

"Not only hospitals, but medical supplies that are being taken to hospitals as well."

"You say the United States is not interested?" Clara asked.

"We have asked several times. They refuse to sign."

"IT'S BEAUTIFUL, DR. APPIA."

"The war in my country was a terrible thing. We are still recovering."

"I know, Miss Barton. I was a doctor in Italy when Napoleon sent his troops. War is terrible. But it is even worse when the injured cannot be treated, when doctors and nurses fear being captured, when medicines are destroyed."

"The Red Cross interests me," Clara said. "I would like to know more about it."

"I shall leave these things with you." Dr. Appia took a pile of pamphlets and clippings from his briefcase and set them on the nearest table.

After the gentlemen left, Clara read the material.

"Your organization sounds like a true help to countries in war," she later told Dr. Appia.

"It is good to hear you say that, Miss Barton. We feel such an organization could be very important in war. And the Red Cross is getting prepared for action. Things look very bad between Prussia and France."

Dr. Appia was right. Two weeks later, the cannons of Germany and France sounded. War had

THE CANNONS OF GERMANY AND FRANCE SOUNDED.

come to Europe. Clara would see the Red Cross in action.

Dr. Appia encouraged Clara to go to Basle, the Swiss town where the Red Cross was headquartered during the war. She agreed.

Clara was impressed by what she saw. Doctors and nurses worked hard. Each day, wagons brought fresh medicine and bandages. The wounded had plenty of food. The hospitals were packed with wounded men, but everything was organized.

"It's marvelous!" Clara exclaimed to a nurse one day. "No matter how fierce the battle grows, you take good care of the wounded. America *must* learn of the Red Cross."

Clara decided to see the Red Cross working at the battlefront. She packed her bags and headed for Strasbourg, a French town being torn apart by German armies.

Clara was asked to take a group of Americans to safety. She would have to go through German lines.

"I will go!" Clara answered. "God will help me."

The people piled into a wagon, pushing and

CLARA WAS IMPRESSED BY WHAT SHE SAW.

shouting. Clara had trouble getting them quiet.

"We will have to pass through German lines," she said. "Because you are Americans, you will be safe. But please let me talk to the guards."

Clara took the American flag she had been given by the doctors at Strasbourg. They told her to show it at each German post.

At the first post, a guard marched up beside the wagon. Clara lifted the American flag so he could see it.

"What is that?" he shouted.

"Why. . .why, it's the American flag," Clara stammered.

"I don't believe you. Hand it to me."

The soldier pulled it out of Clara's hands and stalked off. After several minutes, he returned.

"This is *not* the American flag. I was in America. I looked at this flag under a good light just to be sure. You are under arrest!"

"But you're making a mistake," Clara argued. "Where did you go in America?"

"Mostly in Mexico."

"WHAT IS THAT?"

"They have their own flag. Isn't there some way you can check this?"

"All right, I shall see if this flag is listed in the books we have." Once again, the guard marched away.

Clara turned to the people in the wagon. Many were crying. "Please do not worry. We will get through."

When the guard returned, he threw the flag in Clara's face.

"I have checked. You may go on. But you are fortunate to have received such kind treatment here."

Clara slapped the reins. As the wagon jerked forward, her passengers cheered.

Clara began thinking of the guard's words. What would happen the next time they were stopped?

An idea flashed through her mind. Clara handed the reins to the man sitting beside her. She got out a needle and thread. Untying the red ribbon from her collar, she formed a cross on her handkerchief. Hastily she sewed it on the sleeve of her dress.

As the wagon lumbered into the next stop, a

SHE GOT OUT A NEEDLE AND THREAD.

guard ran up. When he saw the red cross on her dress, he told Clara to move on.

As the war continued, Clara saw thousands of people helped by the Red Cross. The war stopped, but the Red Cross kept on. It planned how to rebuild damaged areas.

Clara sailed for home, anxious to bring the Red Cross to America.

CLARA SAILED FOR HOME.

CLARA STOOD BEFORE PRESIDENT HAYES.

12

Clara had gotten little rest in Europe. Once she arrived in America, she traveled to a small rest home in Dansville, New York. She would have to be strong before she started fighting for the Red Cross. The fresh air and good food soon made Clara feel much better.

In 1877, Clara stood before President Rutherford B. Hayes. She gave him a letter from the president of the International Red Cross.

"Mr. President, surely you see the value of such an organization. We all hope that war never comes again, but we should be prepared if it does."

President Hayes looked up at Clara. "Miss Barton, I respect your interest in this matter. But don't you feel we would be getting involved with countries far away? It seems to me we should be interested in keeping our own country stable."

"But can't we do both?" Clara argued. "Our world is growing smaller. A man is working on a machine through which we can talk to people miles away. It may work."

"And it may not—just like this Red Cross. A small machine takes only a few dollars to build. But your plan would call for a large amount of money."

"And what is the price of a human life, sir? I have seen the Red Cross save thousands of lives."

President Hayes smiled. "Miss Barton, I suggest you take your letter to the secretary of state. See what he has to say."

The secretary of state agreed with the president. He sent Clara to the assistant secretary of state. Again she was disappointed. But Clara was determined to bring the Red Cross to her country.

In 1880, James Garfield became president. He

PRESIDENT HAYES SMILED.

was a friend of Clara's from the war.

"Surely you recall the horrible days of battle, Mr. President," Clara said to him. "Please read this letter and see if you don't find value in the Red Cross."

Clara watched President Garfield read the letter. He returned the letter and shook her hand.

"Those battlefields were sights I can never forget, Miss Barton. I remember a boy who was shot as he stood just a few inches from me."

"I saw many boys like that," Clara said.

"Miss Barton, I like this plan. Naturally you will have to see the secretary of state. He must have his say on matters involving other countries."

Clara looked down.

"Now, Miss Barton, I mean what I say. I do like this plan. I will relay to Secretary Blaine my feelings. He will expect you, and I'm sure you two will get along fine."

Secretary Blaine welcomed Clara warmly. He too liked the idea.

It had taken almost five years, but Clara had

PRESIDENT GARFIELD READ THE LETTER.

convinced the officials of her country to believe in the Red Cross program.

The Red Cross treaty sped through Congress. Everywhere people were talking about the new organization. Once the president signed the treaty, Clara could officially begin making plans.

President Garfield called her to the White House.

"Surely you will become the first president of the Red Cross," Clara said. "It's an honor due you as head of the country."

"No, it is an honor due *you* for the work you have done. Without you, there would be no Red Cross. You must organize and lead the group."

Sixty-five-year-old Clara accepted the new job.

That July, as Clara was riding in a carriage, she noticed people running. She asked the driver to stop. Stepping down from the carriage, Clara stopped a woman who was crying.

"What's wrong?" Clara asked.

"It's the president. He's been shot!"

Clara climbed into her carriage and ordered the

"WITHOUT YOU, THERE WOULD BE NO RED CROSS."

driver to return home. She prayed for the president's recovery.

For months, the president lingered between life and death. But on September 19, 1881, President Garfield died.

Sadly Clara returned to Dansville. Her hopes for an American Red Cross dimmed. Wasn't this the role the Lord had chosen for her? Had she failed Him?

Within weeks, Clara had the answer. The new president, Chester Arthur, invited her to the White House.

"President Garfield told me of the plans for the Red Cross, Miss Barton. I see no reason these plans should not be carried out."

Clara could almost hear the words of Mark 4:40: *Why are ye so fearful? How is it that ye have no faith?*

Newspapers soon criticized Clara. Many people thought it was wrong for a woman to have so much publicity. "This Barton person is merely seeking to make herself famous," wrote one editor. "This is a man's work," observed another.

But on July 26, 1882, the United States joined

NEWSPAPERS CRITICIZED CLARA.

the International Red Cross. The American Red Cross soon blazed into action.

A forest fire raged across Michigan. People were homeless and starving. An urgent plea for help reached the American Red Cross. Clara saw that the plea was answered. Soon letters of gratitude poured in:

> *Dear Miss Barton,*
>
> *We lost our whole farm in the fire. All our stock was killed. If it had not been for the help you sent us, we could never have survived. God bless you, dear saint. We are now building our house again. We will make it, thanks to you.*
>
> *Forever your servant,*
> *Hannah Mills*

Julian B. Hubbell, a medical student, offered his services as a field agent for the Red Cross. His family was wealthy. He requested no salary. "My payment will come from being useful to so humane and Christian an organization as the Red Cross," he

A FOREST FIRE RAGED ACROSS MICHIGAN.

said. Clara accepted his offer.

Clara soon heard from an old friend, Benjamin Butler. As a Union general, he had supported Clara on the battlefields. Now he was governor of Massachusetts. He invited Clara to visit him. She went at once.

"You have probably heard of the efforts of Miss Dorothea Dix to improve the lot of those unfortunates in our country's prisons," the old general began. "I'm hoping you might help us with such an effort here in Massachusetts."

"Me?" Clara exclaimed. "But I know nothing about prisons."

"You know a great deal about humane treatment and service to others. I would like you to serve as superintendent of the Women's Reformatory Prison at Sherborn."

Give me your direction, O God, she prayed. *Is this a path You would have me follow?* For several minutes she was silent.

"If you think it is a job I can do," she said to the governor, "I will accept. But I must insist that I

"ME?" CLARA EXCLAIMED.

maintain my duties with the Red Cross."

Governor Butler agreed.

In the prison, Clara brought the same kindness she had shown on the battlefields. Each day she visited with the prisoners. A complaint box was put up so the inmates could express themselves.

One guest was amazed that the prisoners could freely visit Clara's office.

"Surely you are too easy with these people," the friend complained. "You are a good Christian woman. Why would you wish to expose yourself to contact with the likes of such individuals?"

Clara smiled. "I thank you for calling me a good Christian woman. I return the compliment twofold, as I have great respect for you. Yet I am surprised that you would raise such a question."

"Surprised? I am sure others would feel the same as I do. The governor undoubtedly recognizes your gift for organization and efficiency, qualities not often given a woman. But surely he does not expect you to have personal visits with the prisoners."

PRISONERS COULD FREELY VISIT CLARA'S OFFICE.

Clara listened, feeling amused and annoyed. Finally she could not restrain herself.

"Governor Butler has given me responsibility for this institution to handle as I deem necessary. To visit personally with the inmates is hardly a torture. If I am not mistaken, one of Jesus' final actions was a promise to a prisoner who suffered the same agonizing death as He did. You haven't forgotten, have you?"

The visitor's gaze fell to the floor.

Clara did everything at the prison. She joined the cooks in the kitchen, stretching limited food supplies. She kept the financial records, working long into the night to cut expenses. She fought for new sewing machines and then set up sewing classes.

One of her favorite activities was talking with the prisoners each morning in the chapel. "There are mistakes in my life, just as there are mistakes in yours," Clara told the women. "Yet we are all blessed with the same God, who is merciful and forgiving. We can turn to Him anywhere, at any time."

The prisoners listened to Clara. They accepted

SHE JOINED THE COOKS IN THE KITCHEN.

her as their friend. One inmate wrote home to her family:

> *Miss Barton gives us hope in tomorrow. I know the Lord must have sent her here. Each day she tells us about someone else who was reclaimed by the Lord. I am going to see her in the morning. She takes special concern about those of us who have large families. She is one grand woman!*

Clara was satisfied with the changes she brought to the prison. But she missed being close to the Red Cross. When she requested a release from her duties, Governor Butler agreed.

"In less than a year, you accomplished what it would have taken anyone else a lifetime to achieve," he told her. "But then, it was no more than I expected from a woman like yourself."

THE LORD MUST HAVE SENT HER HERE.

DEADLY WATERS POURED INTO JOHNSTOWN.

13

Rains pelted the Pennsylvania mountains. The Conemaugh River became an angry snake. But the thirty thousand people of Johnstown felt safe. They were protected by a strong dam.

On May 31, 1889, the dam broke. Deadly waters poured into Johnstown. Within hours, four thousand people were swept away in the water. Houses were pulled from their foundations. The call for help went out.

Clara did not waste a moment. By the first week in June, she was on the scene, wading in mud up to her waist and shouting instructions to Red Cross volunteers.

"This is no place for a lady," General Hastings, the military commander, told her. "We have not recovered all the missing bodies."

"We are here to assist you, General," Clara answered firmly. "We will not be getting in your way, but we might be able to help clear your path."

General Hastings discovered that Clara meant exactly that. Setting up her headquarters in a deserted railroad car, she rolled into action.

Clara set up places for handing out donations. Clothing, food, tools, bedding, furniture, and other supplies poured in from around the nation.

Soup kitchens were set up. Men, women, and children gathered in giant tents to share hot food and news of neighbors.

Carloads of lumber arrived from Illinois and Iowa. Volunteers built homes.

Mr. and Mrs. John Tittle proved to be two of Clara's best helpers. They had a frightening story to tell.

"The flood tore us right out of our home," Mr. Tittle explained. "Thankfully we were together and

SUPPLIES POURED IN FROM AROUND THE NATION.

held hands over the ridgepole of our house as we floated down the river."

"Every time I felt like giving up and letting go, I felt John's hands clasp mine harder," his wife said. "I just kept praying, hoping, and praying some more."

"Someone must have been listening to your prayers," Clara said.

"That's what we believe," John Tittle declared. "Our house floated all the way down to Kernville, where it got hooked onto the bridge. Would you believe that even our dog and parrot were alive inside?"

Mrs. Tittle looked up. "That's why we've come to you, Miss Barton. We prayed that the Lord might spare us. Well, we're here all right, and we'd like to thank Him by helping others."

Clara nodded. "We can use you. There is much to be done."

Although the flood had swept away homes and property, nothing could carry off the spirit of the people. Johnstown began to rebuild. Within weeks,

JOHNSTOWN BEGAN TO REBUILD.

businesses and shops opened. School was held in tents, then moved into actual classrooms.

Once the people were on their feet, the Red Cross needed to leave. "The key to our success is that we appear only as emergency relief and help," Clara told audiences. "Our goal is to provide necessary assistance, to help organize work efforts, to share the donations of others with those who need it most. Never must we be taken as intruders or trespassers. Help and get out–that is our goal."

SCHOOL WAS HELD IN TENTS.

PRESIDENT McKINLEY HAD CALLED ON CLARA.

14

A cool breeze blew across the harbor in Havana.

"Sure you wouldn't like to go below deck, Miss Barton?" a crewman suggested. "A little old lady like yourself shouldn't be standing out here catching cold."

Clara straightened. "Young man, I would recommend *you* to go below deck yourself. There is quite enough wind already without you adding your own."

At seventy-six, Clara was not interested in anyone worrying about her health. It was 1898, and the Spanish had squelched a rebellion by the Cubans. A Cuban request for help reached the United States, and President McKinley had called on Clara.

CLARA BARTON

"What ship might that be?" Clara asked, pointing across the harbor.

"It's the *Maine,*" the crewman answered.

But Clara was far more interested in people. Once she reached shore, she headed directly to the hospitals. What she found shocked her.

Cuban men, women, and children injured in the fighting with Spain lay on floors. Dead bodies remained among the living. Stomachs were bloated from malnutrition.

"The first thing we must do is feed these poor, starving creatures," Clara declared. Quickly she pinned up her floor-length skirts.

"Hardly ladylike!" a nurse murmured.

"There will be many times to be a lady," Clara shot back. "At present, it serves our purposes more if I am able to move swiftly."

Clara turned warehouses into giant food kitchens. For the first time in months, patients were given plenty of good food.

On February 13, Clara was working at her writing table in Havana. Suddenly the room shook. The

"THE FIRST THING WE MUST DO
IS FEED THESE POOR, STARVING CREATURES."

veranda door burst open, revealing a blaze of light.

"It's the *Maine!*" a voice in the hallway shouted. "They've blown up the *Maine!*"

"Merciful God," Clara prayed, "please help us."

Tension filled the air. Were the Spanish responsible for blowing up the *Maine?* People talked of war.

But Clara had no time for such talk. When officials from Washington arrived, she took them to the worst spots on the island. At Artemisa, thousands of Cubans without food and homes roamed aimlessly.

"This is not the worst of it," Clara said. "We have already lost three thousand from starvation and inadequate care."

"Do what you must do," the officials told Clara. "We shall carry the word back home, and you shall receive support."

Clara became a human hurricane, seeing that new hospitals were set up in warehouses, supervising food rationing, getting Cuban officials to enforce new laws. Food, clothing, medicine, and bedding were shipped from the United States.

NEW HOSPITALS WERE SET UP.

CLARA BARTON

On April 25, 1898, war was declared between the United States and Spain. Fearing for her volunteers, Clara moved Red Cross headquarters to Tampa, Florida.

Some Washington officials were afraid supplies might end up in enemy hands. Clara persuaded officials that her work was essential. President McKinley ordered all government agencies and offices to give full recognition to the Red Cross and to use its services.

Jubilant, Clara headed back into action. Loaded with vital supplies, the *State of Texas* sailed to Cuba.

The *State of Texas* anchored in Guantanamo, where the U.S. Marines were in control. An urgent request came for Clara to journey to the battlefront.

"She's in her seventies," one physician argued. "We can't ask her to travel so close to the fighting."

"You don't know Clara Barton," another official said. "That is where she feels most at home."

The decision was made. Clara left for the front in a hay wagon.

"It will be a bumpy ride," the driver told her.

THE U.S. MARINES WERE IN CONTROL.

CLARA BARTON

"All I care about is arriving safely," she answered.

Clara found three giant tents with operating tables, surrounded by smaller tents for the wounded soldiers. Men lay in soaking grass. The sun blazed down on them during the daytime, while chilly dew covered them at night.

Clara headed first to the cookhouse. She built a fireplace and ordered big kettles scrubbed and cleaned. Then she began making gruel. The aroma caused the wounded to cry out.

"Miss Barton is here! We'll get some decent food."

She had no blankets, so Clara tore strips of muslin to cover the patients. She saw that the wounded received her famous "Red Cross cider," made from stewed apples, prunes, and lime juice.

One night as Clara helped a surgeon operate, a shot rang out. Clara felt a body lean against her. She lowered the staff member's body to the ground. His bullet wound was fatal. Clara closed the man's eyes, tears coming to her own. She removed the body from the area. Then she returned to her position at

CLARA HELPED A SURGEON OPERATE.

the operating table.

More Red Cross volunteers joined Clara in Cuba. But an outbreak of yellow fever added new problems. Officials feared people would spread the disease. Clara, recognizing the importance of supplies reaching the starving people in Santiago, insisted on sailing to shore.

Clara continued directing Red Cross services in Cuba. By the time she sailed for home in November 1899, her organization had distributed six thousand tons of supplies.

"When history books record the American victory over Spain in this campaign," President McKinley wrote Clara, "you deserve mention among our finest soldiers."

PRESIDENT McKINLEY WROTE CLARA A LETTER.

"THERE, IT IS DONE."

15

With a firm hand, Clara signed her name. She folded the document and slid it into an envelope. "There, it is done," she murmured softly.

Clara leaned back in her chair. She knew about the arguing within the American Red Cross.

"She's just too old, too demanding."

"It wouldn't be so bad, but she's so bossy. Everything must be done her way."

Some people felt Clara was no longer the right person to be running the American Red Cross. At eighty-four, she had held the position for twenty-three years.

"Do you have any mail to go out today?" A

young girl stood at the doorway.

"Yes," Clara answered, holding up the envelope. "Indeed I do."

Newspaper headlines carried the story of Clara Barton's resignation as president of the American Red Cross. She wrote to her nephew Stephen:

> *I am the last of my generation—I am strange among the new. We cannot comprehend each other. I have lacked the knowledge of the newer generation, and done my work badly, and naturally grow discouraged and timid and want to escape it all. . . .*

Stephen hurried to Clara's home. She enjoyed his visits. He encouraged her to share stories from her childhood. Eagerly she wrote *The Story of My Childhood* for young readers.

One afternoon, Clara sat in the garden enjoying the sunset. She heard a noise behind her. Turning, she saw a stranger approaching.

"Miss Barton? Is it really you?"

Clara stared at the man. His hair was white and

CLARA SAT IN THE GARDEN.

shaggy. His brown suit was faded and worn. But there was something familiar about him. "I'm sorry. I don't seem able to remember your name."

"I wouldn't expect you to, Miss Barton. Guess you just knew me by Pete. It was a long time ago."

"Pete!" Clara exclaimed. "I remember. It was at Harpers Ferry. You drove the wagon to Harpers Ferry. We had to travel by night so we could pass the other wagons. Yes, I do remember. You were about the best driver I'd ever seen."

Pete sat down on the bench beside Clara. "It was about fifty years ago, Miss Barton. It's amazing that you would remember me."

"I will never forget those days."

Pete pulled out a crumpled scrap of paper from his coat and handed it to Clara.

"I want you to have this, Miss Barton. I got it from my son while he was in Cuba a few years ago during the Spanish-American War. Thought you might like to read it."

"You read it to me, Pete. My eyes are not as good as they once were."

"Glad to, Miss Barton." He read:

THERE WAS SOMETHING FAMILIAR ABOUT HIM.

CLARA BARTON

Dear Dad,

Just wanted you to know I am safe here and feeling fine. I'm getting rid of this fever fast. The fighting is letting up, and I think I'll be coming home soon.

By the way, Dad, you know that Miss Clara Barton you always talk about from your war days? Well, would you believe she's down here in Cuba? She moves faster than anybody else and she's even made the food eatable. They still call her the "angel of the battlefield." I can understand why!

That's about all for now, Dad. Take good care of yourself.

Your son,
Richard

"It's a lovely letter," Clara said.

"He's a fine boy, Miss Barton. Lives right next door to me. Never given me a bad moment—not like so many young folks these days."

"It is a changing world, isn't it, Pete?"

"You haven't changed much, Miss Barton. Still

"IT IS A CHANGING WORLD, ISN'T IT, PETE?"

small and feisty, aren't you?"

Clara shook her head. "Small, perhaps, but not quite as feisty. I feel the years, Pete."

He smiled. "Some days, I do. But I'm reminded of the words of the Good Book, Miss Barton. Remember Job 42:12? 'So the Lord blessed the latter end of Job more than his beginning.' And Proverbs 16:31: 'The hoary head is a crown of glory.' "

Clara sat in silence. For so long the troubles of the Red Cross had filled her mind. She had allowed the worries of this world to weigh her down.

Clara took Pete's hand. "You have been a welcome visitor, good friend. Surely the Lord directed your footsteps to me. Now, I baked a fresh apple pie this morning. Would you stay and help me eat it?"

"Will there be any Red Cross cider to wash it down with?" Pete asked, his eyes teasing.

"We shall look," Clara answered.

Slowly the two of them walked into the house, stopping to glance up at the red, white, and blue of the United States flag, and at the red cross on the white banner flying overhead.

THEY GLANCED AT THE FLAG OF THE RED CROSS.

SHE WROTE THE HISTORY OF THE RED CROSS.

16

"Make sure you tie that securely, Miss Barton," the gardener said.

Clara tied the plant bud carefully. She rose to her feet and dusted off her skirt.

At eighty-nine, Clara was taking on a new challenge. She was learning how to graft trees. That same month—April 1911—she'd finished writing *The History of the Red Cross*.

"There are too many people who act ninety when they are but fifty," Clara wrote to a friend. "I, too, feel the pains and aches of age, but there is still much to do before I go to meet my loving Creator."

Clara wrote her will and drew up instructions for her funeral. Her horse, Baba, was to be sent to a friend in Virginia.

Clara surrounded herself with books. She enjoyed the Greek stories of victories over great odds.

"Perhaps you enjoy reading of such conquests since you had so many battles of your own," her friend, Dr. Julian Hubbell, observed.

Clara shook her head. "My battles were small. How often I think of those boys on the bloody battlefields. Many of them uttered no complaint, yet they lay in mortal pain."

In July, a box arrived. It was a surprise gift from an unknown admirer.

"Oh, my!" Clara exclaimed when she opened the box. "It's a typewriter. I have no idea how such a machine works."

"If I know you, you will learn with great speed," Dr. Hubbell said.

"I shall give it my best," Clara said.

She studied the directions carefully. Within two hours she finished a typewritten letter. "You must

SHE FINISHED A TYPEWRITTEN LETTER.

pardon the mistakes," she pleaded. "The meeting of an old woman and a young machine does not always lead to favorable results."

Autumn brought pain, but Clara's spirits rallied as Christmas approached.

"I am feeling much better today," she told a reporter in mid-December, "and have every hope of spending a pleasant and joyful Christmas when I shall celebrate my ninetieth birthday."

Clara *did* enjoy her birthday. Friends and relatives visited. As Clara gazed across the room at a small nativity scene, her lined face brightened.

"Would you believe there are those who feel sorry for us who must share our birthdays with the Savior?" she asked. "What greater joy could one ask for a birthday?"

With the new year, Clara sensed her life was ending. In a final letter to her friend, the Grand Duchess of Baden, Clara said farewell:

Dearest, dearest Grand Duchess,
   They tell me I am changing worlds, and

CLARA GAZED ACROSS THE ROOM AT
A SMALL NATIVITY SCENE.

one of my last thoughts and wishes is to tell
you of my unchanging love and devotion to
you. I have waited long to be able to tell
you of better news, but it does not come.

Thanks, oh, thanks for your letters and
your love. Dr. Hubbell will write you of me
when I am gone and I commend him to you.
May God bless and keep you forever more.

Blessings ever,
Clara Barton

April came with the joyful tidings of Easter. On April 10, Clara had a dream that brought Dr. Hubbell and her nephew Stephen to her bedside. She sat up, her back braced against pillows.

"I thought I was on the battlefield," Clara said. "The poor boys were lying on the cold ground with no nurses and no physicians to do anything for them. I saw surgeons coming, and too much was needed by all of them to give special attention to anyone. Then I woke to hear myself groan because I have a stupid pain in my back. Here on a good bed with every

"I THOUGHT I WAS ON THE BATTLEFIELD."

attention! I am ashamed that I murmur!"

Clara had little time left for murmuring. On April 12, 1912, with Dr. Hubbell and Stephen beside her, she said her last words. "Let me go!"

News of Clara Barton's death captured newspaper headlines around the world. In keeping with her wishes, the funeral ceremony was simple.

Clara's body was taken back to Massachusetts for burial. Dr. Hubbell and Stephen hired a covered express wagon for part of the journey.

"It's a sorry night for such a mission," the wagon driver remarked, peering through the thick fog. "Will you be taking the lady far?"

"Miss Barton is to be buried in North Oxford, Massachusetts," Dr. Hubbell replied quietly.

"Is this the body of Clara Barton?" the driver exclaimed. "Why, my father was a Confederate soldier, and at the battle of Antietam he was wounded in the neck and was bleeding to death when Miss Barton found him and bound up his wounds."

Soldiers waited at the city of Worcester, Massachusetts, to accompany the body to Oxford. Veterans,

NEWS OF CLARA'S DEATH
CAPTURED HEADLINES IN NEWSPAPERS.

friends, and relatives gathered to share their stories of Clara. As her body was buried beside the graves of her mother and father, the song "Jesus, Lover of My Soul" carried along the warm spring breezes:

Jesus, lover of my soul, Let me to Thy
*   bosom fly,*
While the nearer waters roll, While the
*   tempest still is high!*
Hide me, O my Savior, hide, Till the storm
*   of life is past;*
Safe into the haven guide, O receive my
*   soul at last!*

Other refuge have I none–Hangs my
*   helpless soul on Thee;*
Leave, O, leave me not alone, Still support
*   and comfort me!*
All my trust on Thee is stayed, All my help
*   from Thee I bring;*
Cover my defenseless head, With the
*   shadow of Thy wing.*

"JESUS, LOVER OF MY SOUL" CARRIED ALONG THE WARM SPRING BREEZES.

CLARA BARTON

*Thou, O Christ, art all I want, More than
    all in Thee I find;*
*Raise the fallen, cheer the faint, Heal the
    sick and lead the blind.*
*Just and holy is Thy Name: I am all
    unrighteousness;*
*False and full of sin I am, Thou are full of
    truth and grace.*

*Plenteous grace with Thee is found, Grace
    to cover all my sin;*
*Let the healing streams abound, Make and
    keep me pure within.*
*Thou of life the fountain art, Freely let me
    take of Thee;*
*Spring Thou up within my heart, Rise to
    all eternity.*

"JUST AND HOLY IS THY NAME."